This book belongs to:

HAWAIIAN WORD BOOK just for Kids

Illustrated by Lance Bowen

BeachHouse

The Hawaiian Alphabet

The Hawaiian alphabet consists of thirteen letters:

five vowels—a, e, i, o, u
eight consonants—h, k, l, m, n, p, w,
and the 'okina (') which is considered a consonant

The 'okina sounds like the glottal stop that occurs between "oh-oh."
The vowels have two sounds, unstressed and stressed, as follows:

a, as in water   **ā,** as in ah
e, as in wet   **ē,** as in hey
i, as in bit   **ī,** as in police
o, as in obey   **ō,** as in bow
u, as in pull   **ū,** as in spoon

Stressed vowels have a kahako (¯) over them.
Two vowel combinations usually merge as a diphthong,
some examples being:

ou, as in soul   **ai,** like "i" in light
oi, as in loiter   **au,** like "ou" in out
ae, like "y" in my   **ao,** like "ow" in how
ei, as in veil

Pluralize

There is no "s" in the Hawaiian language; to pluralize a word,
you would put **nā** before the word. For example:

pua—flower   **maka**—eye   **'īlio**—dog
nā pua—flowers   **nā maka**—eyes   **nā 'īlio**—dogs

There are other ways to pluralize,
but this is the easiest rule for beginners.

Information from
The Hawaiian Word Book
by Jade Mapuana Riley,
courtesy of Mutual Publishing, LLC.

My 'Ohana (Family)

mom
makuahine

bird
manu

brother
kaikunāne
kaikua'ana
kaikaina

baby
pēpē

cousin
hoahānau

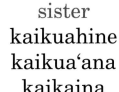

sister
kaikuahine
kaikua'ana
kaikaina

dog
'īlio

auntie
'anakē

dad
makua
kāne

cat
pōpoki

child
keiki

grandma & grandpa
kupuna wahine & kupuna kāne

uncle
'anakala

Look at Me!

head
po'o

hair
lauoho

eyes
maka

ear
pepeiao

nose
ihu

chin
'auwae

mouth
waha

arm
lima

chest
umauma

elbow
ku'eku'e

stomach
'ōpū

hand
lima

leg
wāwae

knee
kuli

foot
wāwae

toe
manamana
wāwae

swimsuit
lole ʻauʻau

Time to Get Dressed

shorts
lole wāwae pōkole

sunglasses
makaaniani lā

hat
pāpale

socks
kākini

t-shirt
pālule

dress
lole

raincoat
kuka ua

aloha shirt
palaka aloha

shoes
kāmaʻa

pajamas
lole moe pō

slippers
kalipa

bed
moe

mirror
aniani

plant
mea kanu

window
pukaaniani

quilt
kapa kuiki

lamp
kukui

desk
pākaukau hana

table
pākaukau

sofa
kokī

chair
noho

door
puka

rug
moena weleweka

In My Hale (house)

In the Kitchen

microwave
'omawawe

refrigerator
pahu hau

dish towel
kāwele pā

cupboards
pahu pā

sink
kinika

toaster
mea ho'opāpa'a
palaoa

sponge
hu'akai

sauce pan
ipuhao hana kai

knife
pahi

spoon
puna

bowl
'umeke

fork
'ō

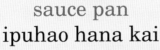

frying pan
pā palai

oven
'oma

plate
pā

pots
ipu hao

blocks
palaka

book
puke

chalkboard
papa ‘ele‘ele

backpack
pāiki hā‘awe

globe
poepoe honua

School is Cool

flag
hae

paint
pena kuapapa wai

pencil
penikala

teacher
kumu kula

chair
noho

scissors
‘ūpā

puzzle
nane ‘āpana

red
'ula'ula

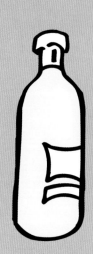

yellow
melemele

pink
'ākala

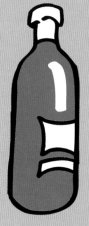

blue
uliuli

orange
'alani

purple
poni

black
'ele'ele

A Rainbow of Colors

white
ke'oke'o

green
'ōma'oma'o

one
'ekahi

two
'elua

three
'ekolu

four
'ehā

five
'elima

six
'eono

seven
'ehiku

eight
'ewalu

nine
'eiwa

ten
'umi

Counting 1, 2, 3

basket
'eke

vegetables
lau'ai

milk
waiū

candy
kanakē

carrots
kāloke

fruit
hua

purse
pāiki

juice
wai

Trip to the Market

money
kālā

can
kini

bag
'eke

wagon
ka'a

rake
hao kope

bird
manu

butterfly
pulelehua

hibiscus
aloalo

ant
naonao

plumeria
melia

umbrella
māmalu

frog
poloka

swing
lele

cockroach
ʻelelū

palm tree
kumu niu

gecko
moʻo

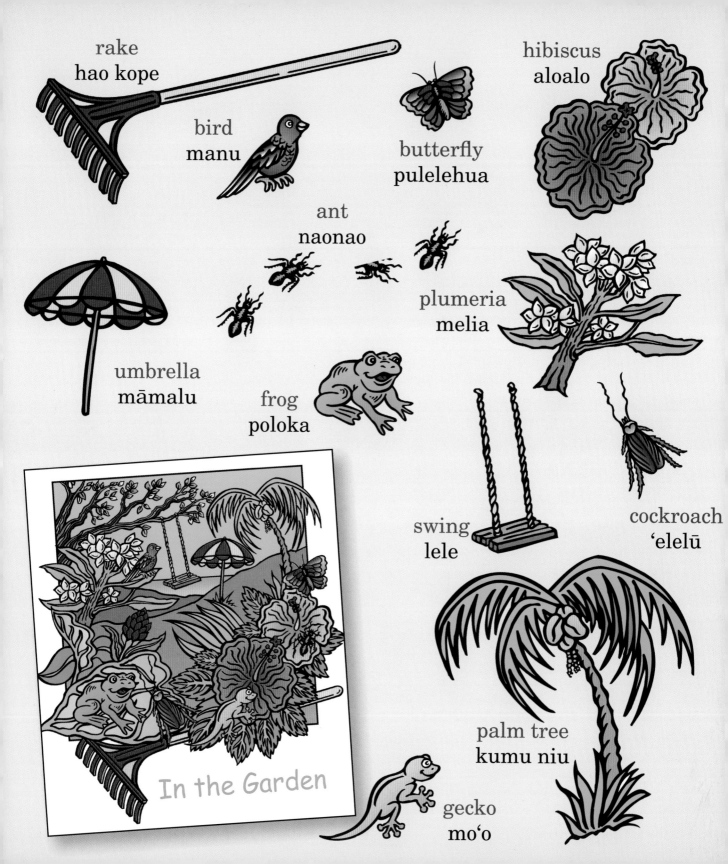

In the Garden

goat
kao

tractor
kaʻa kauō

rooster
moa kāne

crops
mea hoʻoulu

seeds
ʻanoʻano

shovel
kopalā

chicken
moa

pig
puaʻa

barn
hale holoholona

PURE SEED

On the Farm

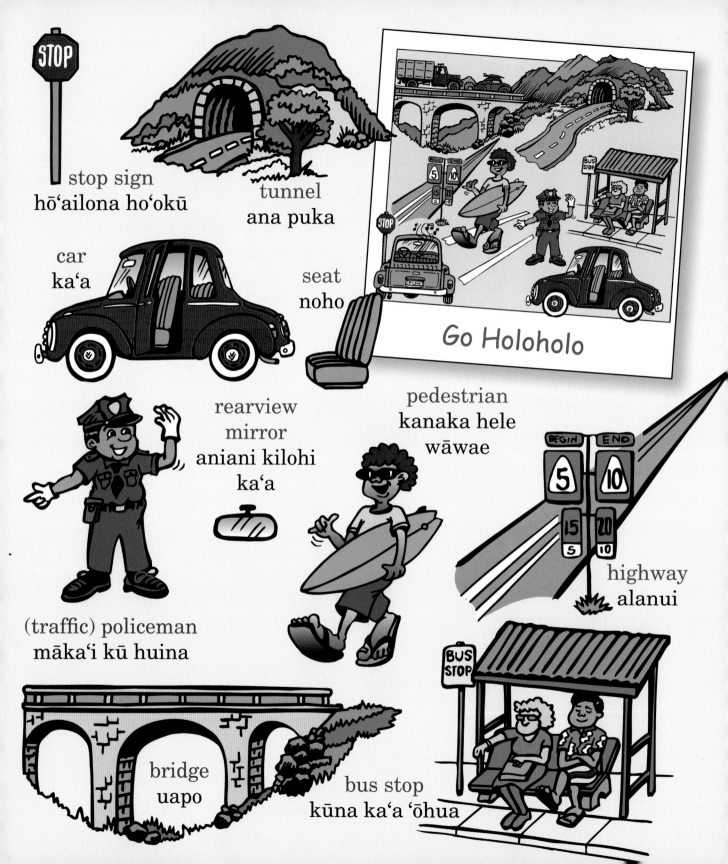

stop sign
hōʻailona hoʻokū

tunnel
ana puka

car
kaʻa

seat
noho

Go Holoholo

rearview
mirror
aniani kilohi
kaʻa

pedestrian
kanaka hele
wāwae

highway
alanui

(traffic) policeman
mākaʻi kū huina

bridge
uapo

bus stop
kūna kaʻa ʻōhua

STOP

BEGIN END
5 10
15 20
5 10

BUS
STOP

motorcycle
mokokaikala

baby stroller
kaʻapēpē

truck
kalaka

Things That Go

skates
kāmaʻa holo paheʻe

bus
kaʻa ʻōhua

taxi
kaʻa hoʻolimalima

skateboard
papa huila

bicycle
paikikala

train
kaʻaahi

flower garland
lei

rainbow
ānuenue

volcano
lua pele

waterfall
wailele

pier
uwapo

hula
hula

Only in Hawai'i

cliff
pali

Diamond Head
Lē'ahi

canoe
wa'a

beach
kahakai

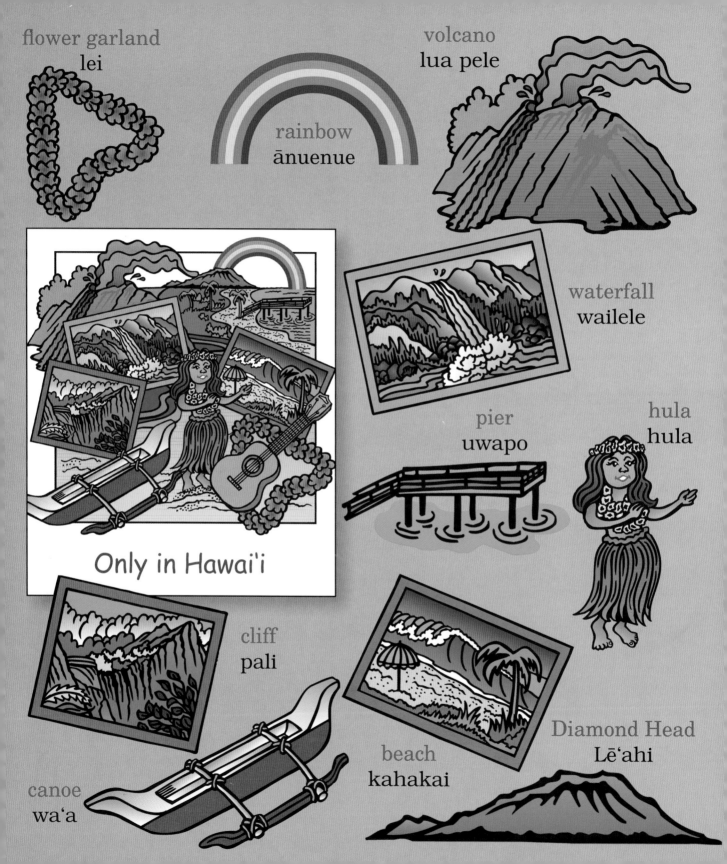

drum
pahu

gourd
ipu

chanter
mea oli

guitar
kīkā

singer
pu'ukani

Let's Make Music

conch shell
pū

gourd
rattle
'ulī'ulī

'ukulele
'ukulele

hula dancer
mea hula

cow
pipi wahine

lion
liona

panda
pea Kina

duck
koloa

peacock
pīkake

elephant
'elepani

orangutan
'oulanakana

snake
naheka

turtle
honu
pahu

monkey
keko

tiger
kika

giraffe
kilape

Going to the Zoo

swimming
'au

windsurfing
holo papa pe'a

paddling
hoe

Makai (Ocean)

surfing
he'e nalu

fishing
lawai'a

scuba diving
lu'u kini ea

kayaking
wa'a kaiaka

sailing
holona

Let's Eat Out

paper napkins
kāwele pepa

menu
papa kuhikuhi
mea 'ai

shoyu
(soy sauce)
koiū

salt
pa'akai

chopsticks
lā'au 'ai

pepper
pepa

bill
palapala kū'ai

waitress
wahine lawelawe

restaurant
hale 'aina

rice
laiki

banana
mai'a

pineapple
hala kahiki

eggs
hua

chicken
moa

mango
manakō

poi
poi

shave ice
haukōhi

papaya
mīkana

mochi
mōchī

bread
palaoa

'Ono Grinds

towel
kāwele

crab
pāpaʻi

shell
pūpū

sandcastle
kākela one

ball
kinipōpō

facemask
makaaniani luʻu

mat
moena

slippers
kalipa

bucket
pākeke

surfboard
papa heʻe nalu

shovel
kopalā

At the Beach

boat
moku

fish
i'a

turtle
honu

coral
puna

Things in the Ocean

shark
manō

canoe
wa'a

dolphin
nai'a

surfer
he'e nalu

jellyfish
pololia

whale
koholā

starfish
pe'a

seaweed
limu

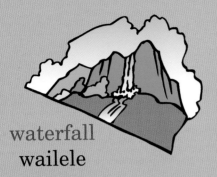

waterfall
wailele

backpack
pāiki hāʻawe

arrow
nahau

map
palapala ʻāina

water bottle
ipu wai

rope
kaula

mountain
kuahiwi

compass
pānānā

boots
puki

Go Take a Hike

rainforest
maʻukele

walking
stick
koʻokoʻo

cave
ana

Hawai'i's Special Animals

whale
koholā

gecko
mo'o

parrot
manu aloha

dolphin
nai'a

peacock
pīkake

horse
lio

mongoose
manakuke

goose
nēnē

seal
'īlioholoikauaua

turtle
honu

hat
pāpale

scrip
kikiki

clown
mea hoʻomākeʻaka

Fun at the Fair

balloons
pāluna

prize
makana

popcorn
kūlina
pohāpohā

shave ice
haukōhi

carousel horse
lio laʻau

roller coaster
kaʻa lola

bull
pipi kāne

lasso
kaula hoʻolei

cowboy
paniolo

saddle
noho lio

pony
pone

horseshoe
kāmaʻa hao

dog
ʻīlio

hay
mauʻu maloʻo

cows
pipi wahine

horse
lio

Paniolo Days

television
kīwī

cd
sēdē

computer
kamepiula

Get Plugged In

calculator
mīkini helu

camera
pahupaʻikiʻi

keyboard
papa pihi kamepiula

radio
lēkiō

laptop
kamepiula lawelima

telephone
kelepona

mirror
aniani

toilet paper
pepa hāleu

soap
kopa

toilet
lua

shower
kililau

Bathtime!

toothbrush
palaki niho

hairbrush
palaki lauoho

toothpaste
pauka niho

bath towel
kāwele ʻauʻau

bath tub
kapu ʻauʻau

razor
pahi
ʻumiʻumi

shower curtain
pale kililau

Bedtime

moon
mahina

stars
hōkū

book
puke

toys
mea pā'ani

teddy bear
pea ki'i

pillow
uluna

window
pukaaniani

blanket
kapa moe

lamp
kukui

telescope
'ohe nānā

pajamas
lole moe pō

bed
moe

shadow
aka

mirror
aniani

toilet paper
pepa hāleu

soap
kopa

Bathtime!

toilet
lua

toothbrush
palaki niho

toothpaste
pauka niho

shower
kililau

hairbrush
palaki lauoho

bath towel
kāwele ʻauʻau

bath tub
kapu ʻauʻau

razor
pahi
ʻumiʻumi

shower curtain
pale kililau

Bedtime

moon
mahina

stars
hōkū

book
puke

toys
mea pā'ani

teddy bear
pea ki'i

pillow
uluna

window
pukaaniani

blanket
kapa moe

lamp
kukui

telescope
'ohe nānā

pajamas
lole moe pō

bed
moe

shadow
aka

Days of the Week

Monday	Pō'akahi
Tuesday	Pō'alua
Wednesday	Pō'akolu
Thursday	Pō'ahā
Friday	Pō'alima
Saturday	Pō'aono
Sunday	Lāpule

Months of the Year

January	'Ianuali
February	Pepeluali
March	Malaki
April	'Apelila
May	Mei
June	Iune
July	Iulai
August	'Aukake
September	Kepakemapa
October	'Okakopa
November	Nowemapa
December	Kēkēmapa

Directions

Toward the mountains	mauka
Toward the sea	makai

Check out these resources to learn more about the Hawaiian language:

Hawaiian Dictionary by Mary Kawena Pukui and Samuel H. Elbert. UH Press.

Māmaka Kaiao, A Modern Hawaiian Vocabulary by Kōmike Hua'olelo, Hale Kuamo'o, and 'Aha Pūnana Leo. UH Press.

www.wehewehe.org

Edited by David Del Rocco

ISBN-10: 1-933067-71-3
ISBN-13: 978-1-933067-71-1

First Printing, September 2015

BeachHouse Publishing, LLC
PO Box 5464
Kāne'ohe, Hawai'i 96744
info@beachhousepublishing.com
www.beachhousepublishing.com

Printed in China